Helping Children See Jesus

ISBN: 978-1-64104-055-6

Conduct of the Church
New Testament Volume 24:
1 Corinthians

Author: R. Iona Lyster
Illustrator: Frances H. Hertzler
Colorization courtesy of Good Life Ministres
Typesetting and Layout: Patricia Pope

© 2018 Bible Visuals International
PO Box 153, Akron, PA 17501-0153
Phone: (717) 859-1131
www.biblevisuals.org

All rights reserved. No part of this publication may be reproduced, stored in a retrieval system or transmitted in any form by any means, electronic, mechanical, photocopy, recording or otherwise, without the prior permission of the publisher, except as provided by USA copyright law.

RELATED ITEMS

To access related items (such as activities, memory verse posters and translated texts) please visit our web store at shop.biblevisuals.org and enter 1024 in the search box on the page.

FREE TEXT DOWNLOAD

To access a FREE printable copy of the teaching text (PDF format) in English or other available languages, enter S1024DL in the search box. Add the item to your cart, and use coupon code XTACSV17 at checkout. Once your order is processed you will receive an email with a link to the free download.

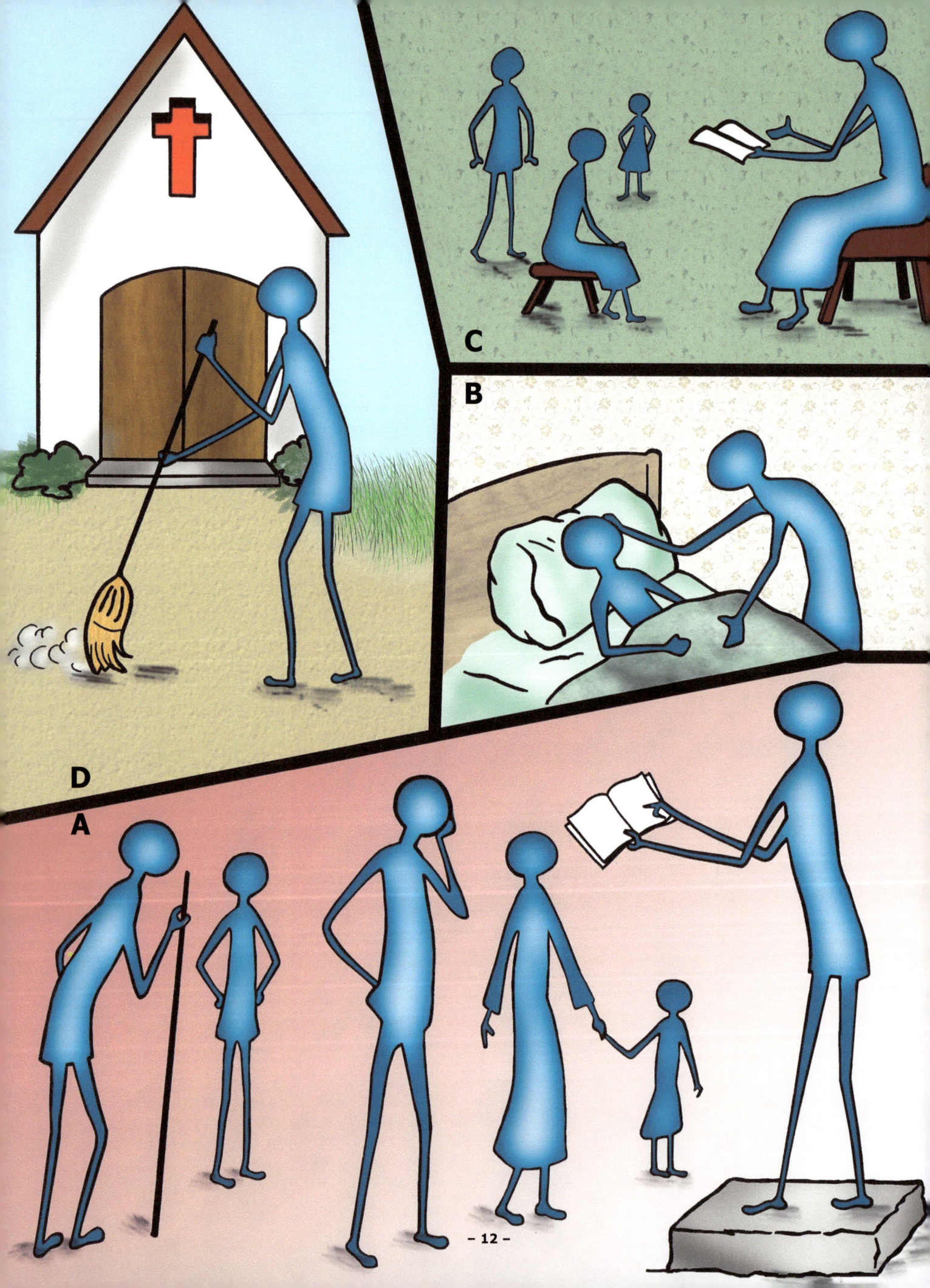

Your body is the temple of the Holy Ghost which is in you . . . you are not your own . . . you are bought with a price: therefore glorify God in your body.

1 Corinthians 6:19-20

Lesson 1
SALVATION–THE REASON FOR RIGHT CONDUCT

NOTE TO THE TEACHER

The adult Corinthian Christians had many problems. So the Apostle Paul wrote First Corinthians to correct these problems. If your students are children, you may feel that they will not be able to understand the adult problems. However, it would be good to read through these lessons before coming to a firm decision.

What were some of the Corinthian problems? They had a very great desire to be wise. (Many children are like this also.) So they had to learn that in Christ alone is true wisdom. Then, too, they were not living as temples of God. They were divided into rival groups. (Have you watched children when they are having games or contests? Do they almost always divide into the same teams? Do they get the feeling that their leader is best and therefore their team is best? If so, they will understand about the divisions in the Corinthian church.)

The Corinthians did not understand that people are married for life. They needed to be taught the correct manner of dress when worshiping God in His house. They had to learn how to participate in the Communion service.

Do you see the importance of teaching these lessons even to children? Remember that the Corinthian believers, though adults, were only children in their new faith in Christ. Yet they had to have strong teaching if they were to become strong Christians.

Scripture to be studied: 1 Corinthians 1-2; Ephesians 2:8-10; 2 Timothy 1:9

The *aim* of the lesson: To help Christians know that because of their wonderful salvation, they should want to live to please God.

What your students should *know*: The Lord Jesus will help believers live lives pleasing to God.

What your students should *feel*: A desire to please God in their daily lives.

What your students should *do*: Ask the Lord Jesus to help them turn from sin. List in their notebooks all their sinful practices and determine how they can turn from those things.

Lesson outline (for the teacher's and students' notebooks):
1. Those who trust in Christ are declared righteous (Romans 3:10-23).
2. Those who trust in Christ are sanctified (1 Corinthians 1:1, 10-13).
3. Those who trust in Christ are redeemed (1 Corinthians 1:9; Ephesians 2:8-10).
4. Believers will be caught up to be with Christ, never again to sin (1 Corinthians 15:51-52; 1 Thessalonians 4:13-18).

The verses to be memorized:

Your body is the temple of the Holy Ghost which is in you . . . and ye are not your own . . . ye are bought with a price: therefore glorify God in your body. (1 Corinthians 6:19-20)

THE LESSON

The Apostle Paul was an excellent missionary. He preached the Gospel wherever he went–in cities, by the seaside, in jails. As soon as people turned to Christ, Paul taught them the truths of God.

Long after Paul left the new Christians, he remembered them. He prayed for them. He wrote letters to them. Some of those letters have been kept for us and form a large part of our New Testament. It is one of his letters, First Corinthians, which we will study in this series. Although Paul wrote the letter more than 1,900 years ago, it is also for us today. (See 1 Corinthians 1:2.) So you will want to listen carefully.

Paul had spent a year and a half in Corinth on his second missionary journey. (See Acts 18:1-17.) He was concerned for that city because it was very wicked. Even though it was one of the richest cities in Greece, the people didn't want to give money to a missionary. So Paul made tents to earn enough to take care of himself while he preached.

By the time he left Corinth, a church had begun. The new believers in that church had been saved, but they were baby Christians. Have you watched babies when they are learning to walk? They take a few steps and fall. Someone helps them to their feet and they try again. Walking, stumbling, falling, and trying again. That is the way it is with baby Christians. They start in their new life but make many mistakes–they sin and fail. The Corinthians were like this. As a result, many problems arose in the Corinthian church. So Paul wrote this letter (during his third missionary journey), explaining the importance of right conduct–that is doing right in the everyday Christian life and doing right in the church.

After the Corinthians turned to Christ and His salvation, they no longer worshiped idols of wood, stone and gold. But there was one thing they treated as if it wase an idol. And that was wisdom. (*Teacher:* Count the number of times that Paul refers to wisdom in the first two chapters of 1 Corinthians. Depending on the ability of your students, you may want to have them read aloud 1 Corinthians 1:17-31, emphasizing the words *wisdom* and *foolishness*.) More than anything else, the Corinthians wanted to be wise. Wisdom! That is what they liked.

So Paul tells the Corinthians (and us) that "God has given us Christ to be our wisdom" (1 Corinthians 1:30). To know Him is to have the knowledge that is most worthwhile. To receive Him as Saviour is to receive His wisdom. What do we get when we receive the wisdom of Christ? We get righteousness, sanctification and redemption.

1. THOSE WHO TRUST IN CHRIST ARE DECLARED RIGHTEOUS
Romans 3:10-23

Show Illustration #1

In our study of the book of Romans we learned what it means to be declared righteous (or justified). When is a person declared righteous? As soon as he trusts in the Lord Jesus Christ who died for him. Why is he/she declared righteous? Because God sees that he/she believes in His Son. No one has any righteousness of his/her own (Romans 3:10-23). Even the best that a person does is like filthy rags in the eyes of God. (See Isaiah 64:6.) But those who trust in the Lord Jesus Christ are justified. So when we have Christ we have His wisdom and are declared righteous.

2. THOSE WHO TRUST IN CHRIST ARE SANCTIFIED
1 Corinthians 1:1-2, 10-13

Show Illustration #2

The wisdom of the Lord Jesus Christ also includes sanctification. We learned the meaning of sanctification in our study of Romans. When is a person sanctified? The moment he/she places his/her trust in the Saviour. The one belonging to Christ is immediately set apart by God for Himself. And God expects the set-apart one to live a life that pleases Him.

Because the Corinthians were baby Christians, they were not always living to please God. The church members were divided into rival groups. Some said they belonged to one particular group. Others said they belonged to other groups. (See 1 Corinthians 1:10-13.) They were using the law against one another. Some had wrong ideas about marriage. Some were ignorant about idol worship. Like babies learning to walk, they were having a hard time doing what was right. Paul knew all this. Still he called the Corinthians *saints* and spoke of their being sanctified in Christ (verse 2).

Did Paul call the Corinthians saints because God was pleased with the things they were doing? No, not at all. In God's sight they were saved and set apart for Him forever. Even though their Christian living was far below God's standard, God saw them as saints (sanctified).

3. THOSE WHO TRUST IN CHRIST ARE REDEEMED
1 Corinthians 1:9; Ephesians 2:8-10

We have seen that because a person trusts in Christ, he/she is declared righteous and is sanctified. Christ is also the believer's redemption. The word *redemption* may not be familiar to you. But the Corinthians knew it well. At the time Paul wrote to them, there were probably more slaves in Corinth than people who were free. (One estimate is that there was a population of 700,000. Of this number, 500,000 may have been slaves.)

Show Illustration #3

A slave owner who wanted to get rid of a slave, simply took him to the slave market and sold him to someone else. So long as a person was a slave, he had nothing to say about his own life. Probably every slave hoped that a day would come when someone would purchase him and set him free. The Word of God speaks of all sinners as slaves. The sinner is a slave of Satan and is controlled by Satan.

But the Lord Jesus Christ purchased those who are bound by sin and set them free forever. The purchase price that He paid is His own precious blood. Because He paid for sinners, He is the Redeemer. The person who places his trust in the Lord Jesus is redeemed–set free from sin and its penalty. This is the meaning of redemption.

Unlike the slaves of old, believers in Christ cannot be returned to the slave market of sin. For when the Lord Jesus bought us with His blood, He set us free forever! Did He do this because of our goodness? No. He did it because He loves us.

Any true Christian is happy that he is no longer a slave of sin. His pardon is so wonderful that sometimes the Christian forgets that this is only part of God's gift of salvation. If our trust is in the Lord Jesus Christ, He *has saved us*. (See 1 Corinthians 1:9; Ephesians 2:8, 9.) We have been pardoned, redeemed, justified and sanctified by God Himself. Because this is so, it should make us want to live lives that please God.

4. BELIEVERS WILL BE CAUGHT UP TO BE WITH CHRIST,
1 Corinthians 15:51-52; 1 Thessalonians 4:13-18

But there is even more to our salvation than our rescue from the penalty of sin. A day will come when *we will be saved* from the presence of sin. Christ died to make it possible for every true Christian to go to Heaven to be with God forever. In Heaven there will be no sin, no sorrow, no suffering. So in First Corinthians Paul says, "Christ will keep you strong until He returns for you. In that day, He will not hold blame against you." (See 1 Corinthians 1:8.)

When will the Lord Jesus return for Christians? We are not told. It may be many years from now, but it could be today!

Show Illustration #4

When He comes, all believers, dead and living, will be caught up to live with Him forever. (See 1 Corinthians 15:51-52; 1 Thessalonians 4:13-18.) There with Him, we shall be like Him, never again to sin. If we truly believe that the Lord Jesus is coming again and that *we shall be saved* from sin, we will want to live for Him now. (See 1 John 3:1-3; Philippians 3:21.)

We *have been saved* from the *penalty* of sin. We *shall be saved* from the *presence* of sin. But there is even more to our salvation. We *are being saved* from the *power* of sin. (See 1 Corinthians 1:18. The English translation should read "unto us *who are being saved*" Also, Jude 24-25.)

Like the Corinthian Christians, we need to be saved once forever by trusting in Christ who died for us. Like them, we need to know all that our wonderful salvation includes. Then we will want to live for God by His power.

If Christ is your Saviour, are you living in such a way that God is pleased with you? Or are you a slave to sin? The Lord Jesus will help you turn away from sin if you let Him. (See 1 Corinthians 10:13.) Will you ask Him to do that right now?

Lesson 2
THE HOLY SPIRIT—THE POWER FOR RIGHT CONDUCT

Scripture to be studied: 1 Corinthians 3-10

The *aim* of the lesson: Christians should yield themselves to the Holy Spirit so they will have power to live correctly.

What your students should *know*: The Holy Spirit lives in and desires to control the lives of those who have put their trust in Jesus Christ.

What your students should *feel*: A desire to let the Spirit of God control their lives.

What your students should *do*: Yield their lives to the Holy Spirit's control. List in their notebooks whatever needs to be yielded to God.

Lesson outline (for the teacher's and students' notebooks):

1. In Old Testament times God dwelt in the Tabernacle (Exodus 25:8; Hebrews 9:1-7).
2. Because all Christians have the Holy Spirit within, they should not be divided into rival groups (1 Corinthians 1:10-17; 3:1-15; John 17:20-21).
3. The indwelling Holy Spirit will help families with their problems (1 Corinthians 7:1-40).
4. The Christian who obeys the Holy Spirit will, like a runner in a race, receive rewards (1 Corinthians 9:19-27; 10:1-33).

The verses to be memorized:

Your body is the temple of the Holy Ghost which is in you . . . and ye are not your own . . . ye are bought with a price: therefore glorify God in your body. (1 Corinthians 6:19-20)

NOTE TO THE TEACHER

When a person trusts in Christ, his/her thinking should be changed, resulting in a definite change in living. The child of God should no longer live to satisfy his/her own desires. He should not live carelessly according to the ways of people who do not know God. That person shouldn't live ignorantly, not knowing what God wants for his/her life. God's purpose is that the Christian should live a godly life, choosing His will.

The moment a person places trust in Christ, the Holy Spirit comes to live within. The Spirit works to fill the believer with Christ's goodness. But the believer must yield to the Holy Spirit and obey Him. Then love, joy, peace and all the fruit of the Spirit can make his life a blessing to himself and to others. (See Galatians 5:22-23.)

Teacher, are you certain that *you* desire to have your life under the control of God the Holy Spirit?

REVIEW QUESTIONS

(*Teacher:* As you review, show illustrations from chapter 1.)

1. In 1 Corinthians 1:30, we're told that the Lord Jesus Christ is the believer's wisdom. And His wisdom includes righteousness, sanctification and redemption. When is a believer in Christ declared righteous (justified) by God? (*The moment a person places his/her trust in Christ as Saviour.*)
2. When a Christian is said to be sanctified, what does it mean? (*It means that because he/she is set apart by God for Himself, he/she should live a life pleasing to God.*)
3. What is meant by the expression that Christ is made unto us redemption? (*He has paid His precious blood to free us forever from our sins. When a person trusts in Him, the Redeemer, that person is redeemed.*)
4. We *have been saved* from the _____ of sin. (*Penalty*) We *are being saved* from the _____ of sin. (*Power*) We *will be saved* from the _____ of sin. (*Presence*)

THE LESSON

The Corinthian Christians loved God and wanted to please Him. But they were like tiny children just learning to walk. Because the Christian life was entirely new to them, it was difficult for them. They stumbled and fell–that is, they sinned and failed–because they had been used to living as other people lived. Before their salvation, they had worshiped idols. They used their bodies for sin. These habits were hard to overcome.

They had to learn–just as we do–that there is One who gives the Christian power to live the right kind of life. That One is the Holy Spirit. Paul wrote, "You are the temple of God, and the Spirit of God lives in you" (1 Corinthians 3:16), and "Your body is the temple of the Holy Spirit who is in you . . . and you are not your own" (1 Corinthians 6:19). Think of that! The Christian's body is the temple of God the Holy Spirit. Could the Corinthian Christians understand that? Yes, indeed.

1. IN OLD TESTAMENT TIMES GOD DWELT IN THE TABERNACLE
Exodus 25:8; Hebrews 9:1-7

Long before Paul wrote his first letter to the Corinthians, long before the Lord Jesus Christ came to earth, God had shown His people what He meant when He said He would live in a temple.

For 40 years the people of God (the Israelites) wandered from Egypt (where they had been slaves) to their new homeland, Canaan. During that time they needed to have a place where they could worship God. So God gave them careful instructions for building a movable place of worship. It was called the Tabernacle. It was a richly furnished tentlike structure that could be carried from place to place. Some years later, after the Israelites had settled down to live in their homeland, they built a permanent place for worship. That was called the temple.

Both the tabernacle and the temple had an outer court where worshiping sinners could come. Each worshiper was required to bring an animal to be sacrificed. The animal took the punishment for the worshiper. That punishment was death. The animal was the sinner's substitute.

Inside the tabernacle and the temple there were two sections. One was the holy place, where priests served God in their worship.

Show Illustration #5

The other section was the most holy place. The high priest was the only one who was allowed to enter the most holy place. He could go in once a year–no more. When he went in, he had to take with him the blood of animals for a sacrifice for his own sins and for the sins of all the people. (See Hebrews 9:7.) God had ordered the most holy place to be built so that He could dwell among His people. (See Exodus 25:8.)

Could the priest see God? No, but he knew God was there because God placed a cloud over the most holy place and filled the inside with His glory. At night the cloud became fire. When the cloud or the fire moved, then the people moved. God was always with His people. (See Exodus 40:34-38.)

So when Paul told the Corinthians that their bodies were the temple of God, they understood that they were His holy dwelling place. (See 1 Corinthians 3:9.) Their bodies belonged to God completely. They understood that God now lives inside His own people, rather than in a building. If you are a believer in the Lord Jesus Christ, your body is the temple of the Holy Spirit. Because this is so, your body should be used to bring honor to God. (See 1 Corinthians 6:20.)

2. BECAUSE ALL CHRISTIANS HAVE THE HOLY SPIRIT WITHIN, THEY SHOULD NOT BE DIVIDED INTO RIVAL GROUPS
1 Corinthians 1:10-17; 3:1-15; John 17:20-21

In many ways the Corinthians were not living the kinds of lives that brought honor to God. They were baby Christians, just learning to live the Christian life. Because they sinned and failed, no one would have guessed that their bodies were God's temple.

Show Illustration #6

For one thing, they were divided into rival groups. Each group claimed that his own group was the best. One said that his group came to know Christ by Paul's preaching. Another supposed that his group was saved because of Apollos. Those in the third group said they were saved through Peter's preaching. (See 1 Corinthians 1:10-17; 3:1-15.) Each group felt that the Christian leader who had led them to Christ was the most important leader. So for that reason, they thought that their particular group was most important. They–the very temple of God–were dividing the Christians into rival groups. What a pity! They had to learn that they all had only one Leader, the Lord Jesus. Paul, Apollos and Peter were all serving Him. God wants His family to be united. They are to love each other. They are to respect one another. Together they are to show the world that they belong to the true God. (See John 17:20-21.) Because the Holy Spirit lives in believers, He is willing to help them to love one another.

3. THE INDWELLING HOLY SPIRIT WILL HELP FAMILIES

1 Corinthians 7:1-40

Show Illustration #7a

The sinning, failing Corinthians had another problem. God wanted one man to be married to one woman. The husband and wife were to belong to each other until one of them died. They were to love one another and be faithful to each other. In such a way they could be a picture of God's love and faithfulness.

The Corinthians, however, were very careless about their marriages. God would help them to overcome this problem if they would let Him. He wanted each believer in a Christian family to live as His holy temple.

Show Illustration #7b

There was another problem in the young Corinthian church. Some of the Corinthians had married unbelievers before they trusted in Christ. Then the saved one tried to lead the unsaved partner to Christ. Often the unsaved one refused to listen to the Gospel and caused trouble. God said that the one who was saved was to be faithful to his or her partner. If children were saved and their parents were not, those children were to honor their parents and try to win them to the Lord. Whether it was the mother, the father or a child who was saved–each was to live as a temple of God's Holy Spirit. By doing so, they might be able to help the unsaved in their families to trust in Christ. The Holy Spirit, who makes the child of God His dwelling place, is ready to help those who ask for His help.

4. THE CHRISTIAN WHO OBEYS THE HOLY SPIRIT WILL, LIKE A RUNNER IN A RACE, RECEIVE REWARDS
1 Corinthians 9:19-27; 10:1-33

Paul wrote that he wanted the Holy Spirit to prepare him to do his best for God. This meant that he would follow God's will for his choices, instead of choosing his own desires and plans. (See 1 Corinthians 9:19-27 and chapter 10.) Because his body was the temple of God, Paul gladly obeyed the One who lived inside him.

Show Illustration #8

Paul explained that life is like a race. Runners in a race, he said, take their training seriously. They run to win a prize. But the prize they win is like leaves on a tree–it doesn't last very long. However, believers who obey the Holy Spirit who lives within them will receive rewards that will last forever.

When a king (or president) comes to live in the home of one of his subjects, that home becomes his palace. Those who live there are eager to keep it fixed up in ways which will please their ruler. No part of that home is kept from him. Everything is exactly as he would like to have it. So it should be with those who are honored by the indwelling of the Holy Spirit. Since the body of the believer is His temple, the believer should want to live a clean and beautiful life–completely under His control.

If your trust is in the Lord Jesus Christ, the Spirit of God is living in you. You are His temple. Have you asked Him to control His dwelling place? If not, will you do so right now?

Lesson 3
CHURCH CONDUCT

> **NOTE TO THE TEACHER**
>
> The word *church* is used in different ways. The building where Christians meet is called a church. A group that meets together in such a building is called a church. The group meeting in Corinth, for example, was called the church in Corinth. All believers since the coming of the Holy Spirit form the true church.
>
> In Corinthians, the true church is called the body of Christ. It is called this to emphasize two things:
>
> 1. The group is one with Christ and with each other. Paul says it is like a human body.
> 2. The purpose of the church group is to speak and to act as Christ did while He was here on earth.
>
> If possible, introduce this lesson by using *The Church* (New Testament 15) to help your students remember the beginnings of the Church.
>
> If you are teaching children, you could begin the lesson this way: "Do people tell you how to behave in church? They want you to be there but often they tell you to stop doing things you like to do. Sometimes they tell you to do things you don't think you want to do. And they don't always do the right things themselves. Or they may disagree with each other about what you should or should not do. Where can you find out what you really can and should do? (*In the Bible, of course*)
>
> "Although the Corinthian Christians were adults when they came to trust Jesus, they didn't know just what to do to please God. Their lives had been entirely different before. So Paul wrote letters to help them and all new Christians to know:
>
> 1. How to live at home to please God
> 2. How to behave in church
>
> "So when we want to know these things, we turn to the Word of God and especially to the book of Corinthians."
>
> If at all possible, write on large paper or a blackboard the outline which is at the end of this lesson. Refer to it as you teach each point. At the conclusion of the lesson, erase one important word in each line. Then review what you have taught by asking the students to complete each statement and write it in their notebooks.

Scripture to be studied: 1 Corinthians 11-14

The *aim* of the lesson: To help all Christians understand that they are given gifts to use for God. They are never to be jealous of others in the church whose gifts may be different.

What your students should *know*: No matter what they do for God, He wants them to do it in a loving way.

What your students should *feel*: A desire to show His love to others.

What your students should *do*: Think of one thing they can do this week to show God's love to someone.

Lesson outline (for the teacher's and students' notebooks):

1. The Lord Jesus Christ is the Head of the Church (1 Corinthians 11:3; Ephesians 1:22; 4:15; 5:23; Colossians 1:18).
2. Proper dress is to be worn in the church (1 Corinthians 11:4-7, 13).
3. Believers are to conduct themselves properly at the Lord's Supper (1 Corinthians 11:17-34).
4. Each believer is needed in the church and has work to do (1 Corinthians 12:1-31).

The verses to be memorized:

Your body is the temple of the Holy Ghost which is in you . . . and ye are not your own . . . ye are bought with a price: therefore glorify God in your body. (1 Corinthians 6:19-20)

THE LESSON

The true temple of God today is not a building. What is His temple? (The body of each believer is the temple of God because the Holy Spirit of God lives there.) We may never be able to understand why the Holy Spirit would be willing to live in believers. But whether or not we understand it, the Bible says it is so. And that is final.

Because each believer is God's temple, all believers together should be a wonderful testimony to unbelievers. Unfortunately this is not always so today. Nor was it always so long ago. God has recorded in the Bible some of the faults of the first churches so that we may learn by their mistakes. The Corinthian church did a number of wrong things. They stumbled and fell like children who are learning to walk. By studying their mistakes, we can learn what we believers should or should not do.

1. THE LORD JESUS CHRIST IS THE HEAD OF THE CHURCH
1 Corinthians 11:3; Ephesians 1:22; 4:15; 5:23; Colossians 1:18

Have you ever thought of how wonderful your human body is? Each part of your body is important–your feet, your legs, your hands, your arms. But which part of your body is the most important? Your lips? Your feet? If you want to pick up a stick, your lips do not say, "Feet, walk over to that stick. Arm, reach out. Hand, pick up the stick." There is, instead, something inside your head that tells your feet to go to the stick, your arm to reach out and your hand to pick it up. Even without thinking, all the parts of your body are under the control of your head. What do you think is the most important part of the human body? The head.

So it is with the Church. God speaks of His church as "the body of Christ." Who is the Head of the body of Christ? The Lord Jesus Christ. Who is the most important part of the body of Christ? The Lord Jesus Christ. Because He is the Head, all the members of His body, the Church, are to obey Him in everything.

How many children are there in your family? (Allow students to answer.) Let's suppose that Mother and Father have to go to the store and leave the children at home. Generally, who would be made responsible for the children while the parents are gone? (*The oldest of the children*)

Show Illustration #9

So it is in the family of God. Christ, the Head, is now in Heaven. Because He is away, He has arranged for certain ones to be responsible for His body (the Church) here on earth. From the time that Eve was tricked by the serpent, God has given this responsibility to men. (See Genesis 3:16.)

In God's eyes, all Christians are equal before Him. (See Galatians 3:26-29.) But His plan is that women are responsible to men. All men are responsible to the men who are church leaders. And the leaders are responsible to God.

Some women may not like to hear that men are the leaders. But God is pleased when women humbly serve Him with men leading. In that way, they are being like the Lord Jesus who humbled Himself. (See Philippians 2:7-8.) He too had One who was His Head. Who was that? God the Father. (See 1 Corinthians 11:3.)

2. PROPER DRESS IS TO BE WORN IN THE CHURCH
1 Corinthians 11:4-7, 13

Show Illustration #10

Have you ever wondered exactly what people should or should not wear when they go to worship God in a church service? The Bible makes it very clear. (*Teacher:* Read 1 Corinthians 11:4, 7.) Men are to have their heads uncovered in church. This is the way they show they are honoring and obeying God.

When women worship, they too can show that they honor and obey God. (*Teacher:* Read 1 Corinthians 11:5-6, 13.) They show their respect for the will of God by having their heads covered in church meetings.

When we first studied about the church, we learned that there are two ceremonies to be practiced. Do you remember what they are? One is baptism. Why are believers baptized? To show others that their trust is now in the Lord Jesus Christ. Apparently the Corinthians were not having a problem with baptism. But they were having trouble over the other ceremony.

3. BELIEVERS ARE TO CONDUCT THEMSELVES PROPERLY AT THE LORD'S SUPPER
1 Corinthians 11:17-34

What is the other ceremony which Christian believers are to practice? The Lord's Supper (which is also called Communion, or the Lord's Table). The Corinthians were doing a number of things wrong when they met around the Lord's Table. (See 1 Corinthians 11:17-34.) From their mistakes we learn that when Christians take part in the Lord's Supper, they are to be in agreement with one another. If they have differences, they should settle them before coming to the table of the Lord. Then, when they meet, their minds can be filled with thoughts of the death and coming again of the Lord Jesus.

Show Illustration #11

The Lord's Supper is to be very simple: a piece of broken bread and a sip of grape juice, representing wine, for each one. It is not a time of feasting, as some of the early Christians thought. They brought food and drink and made a feast instead of using this time to remember the death of the Saviour. This brought shame to the Lord Jesus–the One who was to be remembered.

The Lord's Supper is to be taken thoughtfully and seriously. Some were taking it carelessly and, as a result, they were weak. Others were sick. Some had died. Why? Because they were careless. Taking part in the Lord's Supper is a solemn, serious thing.

4. EACH BELIEVER IS NEEDED IN THE CHURCH AND HAS WORK TO DO
1 Corinthians 12:1-31

Not only is our behavior at the Lord's Supper important. What we do each day is also important. From 1 Corinthians 12, we understand that every person in the body of Christ is important. Our physical bodies have eyes, ears, feet and hands. Each is valuable in a different way. Each is needed. If even the tiniest part is hurt or does not work properly, the whole body hurts and cannot serve in the right way.

So it is in the church. Each person is valuable. Each has some work to do. Whatever God gives a person to do, he (or she) should do it well.

Show Illustration #12a

For some, that work may be preaching.

Show Illustration #12b

For others there is the work of caring for the sick or for those who are old.

Show Illustration #12c

Still others are to be teachers.

Show Illustration #12d

Some may have to do work which no one else may notice–like cleaning in or around the church.

Regardless of what each one does, all in the church must work together, guided by the Head. Who is the Head of the church? The Lord Jesus Christ. (See Ephesians 1:20-23; 4:11-16; Colossians 1:18.)

Because all Christians belong to each other, we dare not be jealous of what others are given to do. In a human body, would a foot be jealous because it is not a hand? Would an ear be jealous because it is not an eye? Each part of the body–foot, hand, ear and eye–is important.

It is the same in God's family. He gives gifts to each one, and He wants each to use them. But more important than the gifts is the way in which the Christian uses His gifts. God wants each of us believers to use our gifts with love. (See 1 Corinthians 13.) The love that pleases Him is the love which makes the Christian kind; love that does not envy: love that does not boast; love that does not get angry; love that does not think evil.

No matter what you do for God, He wants you to do it lovingly. He wants you to show His love to others. Think of some way that you can show His love. Will you ask the Lord right now to help you do that loving act this week?

Teacher: Please write this outline in your notebook.

Church Conduct
1 Corinthians 11-14

1. The Lord Jesus Christ is the Head of the church (1 Corinthians 11:3).

2. Men should be the leaders in the church (1 Corinthians 11:3).
3. Proper dress is to be worn in the church (1 Corinthians 11:14, 15).
   a. Men should have their heads uncovered in church (1 Corinthians 11:4, 7).
   b. Women should have their heads covered in church meetings (1 Corinthians 11:5-6, 13).
4. The proper conduct at the Lord's Supper (1 Corinthians 11:17-34).
   a. Believers should be in agreement with one another (1 Corinthians 11:17-19).
   b. The service is to be simple. The Lord's Supper is a time for remembering what Christ did for us (1 Corinthians 11:20-22).
   c. The service is to be taken seriously (1 Corinthians 11:23-24).
5. Christians receive spiritual gifts (1 Corinthians 12:1-11).
6. All believers in the church are one body (1 Corinthians 12:12-31).
7. Love solves all problems (1 Corinthians 13).

Lesson 4
THE RESURRECTION AFFECTS CHRISTIAN CONDUCT

NOTE TO THE TEACHER

What a wonderful lesson this is to teach! Be sure that you are so happy about it that your students will respond by submitting their lives to God in consistent, loving service.

Before you teach, be sure to read *all* the Scriptures. Remember that there are to be two resurrections: (1) the resurrection of all believers, that they may forever live with God; (2) the resurrection of all unbelievers, that will result in their existing forever away from God. (See John 5:28 and Revelation 20:4-6.) Here, however, just the first resurrection is explained according to 1 Corinthians 15.

After the lesson has been carefully presented, it would be good to ask questions to be certain that the students really understand. Let them ask questions, too, and let them find the answers in Scripture.

You yourself should study carefully what the Bible says (in the last chapters of the Gospels and the first chapter of Acts) about the resurrection body of the Lord Jesus Christ.

Scripture to be studied: 1 Corinthians 15-16; 1 Thessalonians 4:13-18

The *aim* of the lesson: To show that Christians can have in their everyday lives the same power that raised the Lord Jesus from the dead.

What your students should *know*: Because the Lord Jesus arose from the dead, those who believe in Him can have His resurrection power.

What your students should *feel*: A desire to let Jesus be Lord of their lives.

What your students should *do*: Allow the Lord Jesus to be Lord of their lives. Determine what He wants them to do for Him this week.

Lesson outline (for the teacher's and students' notebooks):
1. Jesus Christ rose from the dead (1 Corinthians 15:3-8).
2. Jesus Christ is the *firstfruits*–the first to be raised to endless life (1 Corinthians 15:20; Leviticus 23:9-14).
3. Believers will be given new bodies when Jesus comes for them (1 Corinthians 15:51-52; Philippians 3:20-21; 1 Thessalonians 4:13-18).
4. Jesus Christ is willing to live His life through the lives of believers (Ephesians 1:19-20; 1 Corinthians 15:58).

The verses to be memorized:

Your body is the temple of the Holy Ghost which is in you . . . and ye are not your own . . . ye are bought with a price: therefore glorify God in your body. (1 Corinthians 6:19-20)

REVIEW

1. Long before the Lord Jesus came to earth, God the Holy Spirit dwelt among His people in the most holy place in the temple. Where does He live now? (*In the bodies of those who trust in the Lord Jesus Christ.*)

Show Illustration #6
2. The church in Corinth had several problems. What was one of them? (*They were divided into rival groups, each claiming to be the best.*)

Show Illustration #7a
3. God has planned for one man to be married to one woman. How long is that marriage to continue? (*Until one of them dies*)

Show Illustration #7b
4. If a Christian is married to an unbeliever, what should he do? (*The Christian should try, by a godly life, to lead his/her partner to the Lord.*)

5. Should a Christian make his/her own choices? (No. *The Christian should choose to follow God's will, remembering that his/her body is the temple of God.*)

6. Who is the Head of the church? (*The Lord Jesus Christ*)

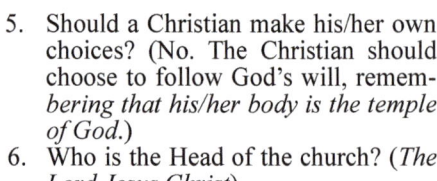

Show Illustration #10
7. In church worship, how should men and women show that they honor God? (*The men should have their heads uncovered; the women should have their heads covered.*)

Show Illustration #11

8. How should the Lord's Supper be observed? (*Simply, thoughtfully, seriously, without feasting*)

9. Because some of the early Christians had been careless at the Lord's Table, what happened to them? (*Some were weak and sickly. Others had died.*)

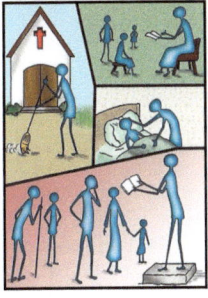

10. Are Christians expected to serve the Lord? (*Yes. Everyone receives gifts from God that make it possible for all to do something for Him. Gifts may differ, but each gift is important.*)

THE LESSON

What is the one thing that most people are afraid of? Old and young, some who are Christians and some who are not, are afraid to die. The person who does not believe in the Lord Jesus Christ should be afraid of death, for it is a fierce enemy—an enemy that separates him/her from God forever.

But the believer, who trusts in the Lord Jesus Christ as Saviour, never needs to be afraid to die. And there is good reason for this, as we will see in our lesson today.

1. JESUS CHRIST ROSE FROM THE DEAD
1 Corinthians 15:3-8

There is one thing that makes Christianity different from all the religions of the world. Each religion was started by someone who died and stayed dead. Christianity was begun by the Lord Jesus Christ who died and did *not* stay dead. He arose and He lives forever.

Show Illustration #13

Because the Lord Jesus rose from the dead, our wonderful Gospel includes three facts:

1. Christ died for our sins.
2. He was buried.
3. He rose again the third day.

(*Teacher:* Point to the appropriate illustration when mentioning each of these three facts.) Let us read together 1 Corinthians 15:3-4. What is meant by the expression: 'according to the Scriptures'? It means that the death and resurrection of the Lord Jesus were promised in the Scriptures even before they occurred. (See Isaiah 53:5-7, 9-10; Luke 18:31-33.)

How do we know that the Lord Jesus rose from the dead? God's Word tells us so, and God's Word is true. The Bible records that scores of people saw Christ after His resurrection. (*Resurrection* is another word for the expression "raised from the dead.") His disciples saw Him, some women saw Him, a group of 500 saw Him at one time. (See 1 Corinthians 15:4-8.)

2. JESUS CHRIST IS THE "FIRST FRUITS"—THE FIRST TO BE RAISED TO ENDLESS LIFE
1 Corinthians 15:20; Leviticus 23:9-14

Perhaps you are thinking, *Yes, I believe the Gospel. I believe that the Lord Jesus Christ rose from the dead. I have received Him as my Saviour from sin. But I am still afraid to die.* Let me tell you that there is good news for you in 1 Corinthians 15:20 which says: "But now is Christ risen from the dead, and become the firstfruits of them that slept."

Do you know what the firstfruits of the harvest are? The people in Corinth would have understood this. Some grain ripens before the rest of the harvest is ready. Usually the first that ripens is the biggest and best grain of the harvest. It is the beginning of the harvest, and it helps the farmer to know that soon the rest of the grain will ripen.

About 1,500 years before Paul wrote to the Corinthian church, God had ordered His people to perform a certain service when their grain began to ripen. Before they themselves used one bit of it, they were to take a sheaf of ripe grain to God's house.

Show Illustration #14

There the priest offered the sheaf to the Lord. (See Leviticus 23:9-14.) They gave their best to God and had His promise of a full harvest later.

So Paul wrote that Christ is "the firstfruits of them that died," that is, Christ was the first to be raised to eternal life. Because Christ rose, we have the promise that all believers will rise from the grave. No true believer, therefore, need ever to be afraid to die. We may not like the thought of dying, but we don't have to be afraid of it. Because the Lord Jesus Christ (the firstfruits) lives, believers (the full harvest) will also live! (See Job 19:25-26.) That is God's promise. It is true.

When will the bodies of believers be raised from their graves? They will be raised when the Lord Jesus comes again. (See 1 Corinthians 15:23.) We don't know the date when He will come again. But He *will* come, for the Bible says so.

3. BELIEVERS WILL BE GIVEN NEW BODIES WHEN JESUS COMES FOR THEM
1 Corinthians 15:51-52; Philippians 3:20-21; 1 Thessalonians 4:13-18

Show Illustration #15

When Jesus comes a trumpet will sound. (See 1 Corinthians 15:51-52.) All Christians who have died will rise from their graves and be caught up to be with Him forever. This is the great harvest, the promised harvest, of all believers. (See also Philippians 3:20-21; 1 Thessalonians 4:13-18.)

What will these bodies be like when they are raised from the grave? The Bible says they will be like Christ's body. (See 1 John 3:2.)

The new bodies will be different from the bodies that went into the ground at the time of death. When grain is planted, it is hard, dry, and dead looking. But deep inside that little kernel is life. It cannot be seen but it is there. In the ground the sun and the rain make the life break through the hard kernel. Finally, at harvest time, the grain is ripe and beautiful and full of life. (See 1 Corinthians 15:35-38; John 12:24.) So it is with the human body. It will be different when it comes up out of the grave, prepared especially to live in the home of God.

It is a wonderful thing to know that the bodies of dead believers will rise when the Lord Jesus comes again. But there is something you must know: many believers will never die. Think of that! The Lord Jesus may come at any time. And when He comes, all Christians who are living will be immediately changed. They will be caught up together with Christ and with those who have been raised from the dead. And they, too, will have resurrection bodies like that of the Lord Jesus. What a day that will be!

The glorious hope of the Christian is to be with Christ in Heaven. But until we have our new bodies like His, and until we are where He is, we have Him here with us. From the moment we place our trust in Him, He comes to live in our hearts. (See Revelation 3:20.) Without Him, we cannot live the Christian life. (See John 15:4, 5.) With Him, even though we may feel we are weak Christians, we can please God.

4. JESUS CHRIST IS WILLING TO LIVE HIS LIFE THROUGH THE LIVES OF BELIEVERS
Ephesians 1:19-20, 1 Corinthians 15:58

Show Illustration #16

The same power that raised the Lord Jesus from the grave is the power that He will give to you if you will invite Him to rule your life. (See Ephesians 1:19-20.) Because He is Lord, He is willing to think through your mind. He wants to speak through your voice. He wants to live His life through you. You do not have to try to imitate Christ. But if you willingly obey Him, He will fill your life with His life.

Perhaps you have been weak and failing like the Corinthian Christians. Instead of having victories in your Christian life, you are being defeated. If that is so, it is because you have not allowed the Lord Jesus to be on the throne of your heart and life. (See Luke 6:46.) You are doing what you want to do, rather than allowing Him to live His life through you.

It is sin not to allow Jesus Christ to be Lord of your life. But there is a way you can correct that. If you will confess your sin, God will forgive you and cleanse your life. (See 1 John 1:9.) Then you will know real joy here on earth.

First Corinthians 15 is perhaps the most important chapter in this book. Whenever you want to know about the resurrection of the Lord Jesus Christ and of believers, turn to this chapter. Remember the last verse of the chapter (verse 58). Because the Lord Jesus rose from the dead and because believers will rise from the dead, we who are His should stand firm. We should always be busy in God's work. Whatever we do for Him will not be wasted, as it would be if there were no resurrection. Are you busy for Him? What do you believe He wants you to do for Him this week?

www.ingramcontent.com/pod-product-compliance
Lightning Source LLC
Chambersburg PA
CBHW060805090426
42736CB00002B/166